Manipulation

How to Get Anybody to Do What You Want

By

Omar Johnson

Copyright 2013 by Omar Johnson. Published by Make Profits Easy LLC

Profitsdaily123@aol.com

facebook.com/MakeProfitsEasy

Table of Contents

Introduction 5
   The Frustration of 'No' 11
Chapter 1 – What is Influence? 13
   Power 17
   Why do People Allow Themselves to be Influenced? 21
Chapter 2 – Defining Your Influence 25
   Do You Have Any Influence? 27
Chapter 3 - A Powerful First Impression 31
Chapter 4 – How to Determine if Someone is Trying to Manipulate You 38
   The Danger Zone 42
   Signs that Someone May be Manipulating You 43
Chapter 5 – Monitoring Your Influence 48
   The Line between Manipulation and Control 49
Chapter 6 – See through People 53
   Understand their True Motivations 54
Chapter 7 – Recognize the 'Bluff' 59
Chapter 8 – Get the Results You Want. Now 63
   Get the Return Phone Call 63
   Get the Job You Want 65
   Get the Promotion 67

Get Someone to Change His or Her Mind..............69

Get People to Open Up to You................................70

Get Forgiveness 71

Stop Abuse Instantly...72

Chapter 9 – Using Manipulation to Influence Change in a Positive Way..74

Introduction

Imagine that you could get anything you wanted in life. Sounds like a dream, doesn't it?

The reality is that the power to accomplish anything you want is well within your reach, if you know how to get things done. When you are able to convince people to do what you want, it gives you an enormous amount of power to accomplish just about any goal or dream that you have.

When people think about the word "manipulation," they almost universally consider it to be a bad word. Manipulation makes people think about getting others to do things that they don't really want to do.

However, manipulation can be a powerful and positive force just as much as it can be a negative force. Being able to convince political leaders to follow through on legislation that can keep the citizens safe and allow them to prosper, even when that legislation goes against a portion of their principles, does that mean that manipulation in this case is a bad thing?

Manipulation, like any form of power, is inherently neutral. Determining whether it is used for good reasons or bad is completely up to the individual who is attempting to apply that manipulative force on to others.

If you want to achieve any number of goals in your life, it is going to require manipulation in some form or another at some time. There is no escaping this inherent truth. The only thing that has to change before you can accomplish your goals is this idea that manipulation is a bad thing.

Just take a moment to think about any number of things that you have achieved, accomplished, or received throughout your life from others and you will find a number of instances in which you used manipulation to get those things. Let me give you a few examples:

- A child wants an ice cream bar on a hot summer day while at the beach. The parent may balk at the idea because he or she doesn't want to spend the money, but the child appears visibly upset, may cry, or cause any other kind of scene because he or she did not get what they wanted. The parent gives in and you have your first example of manipulation. This form of manipulation is a negative one. The child used negative behavior to force his or her parent to make a decision about what behavior they are willing to tolerate at that time.

- How about a more positive example of manipulation? A person applies for a job, gets a call to come in for an interview, so this individual goes into his or her closet and chooses the most stylish, professional, and attractive outfit that he or she can find. Both men and women do this readily, even though women tend to be more obvious examples of this kind of manipulation. When you think about it, how you dress offers subtle signs and indicators to somebody looking to hire you about your character. But do you always dress this way? Most of us do not wear suits when we are on our own outside of work. This is a simple form of manipulation, but it's not a negative one. You are simply looking to make your best impression on your potential future boss.

- Now let's talk about that interview. When you are in interview, you are met with a wide range of questions that can include what are your hobbies, what kind of employee do you consider yourself, or how you might handle a specific situation. Do you answer those questions completely honestly? Do you answer those in an interview the same way you might answer them coming from a family member or friend? Most of us make our best effort to sound impressive during an interview. Why? We are trying to manipulate the interviewer into seeing that we are ideally suited for the job that is being offered.

As you can see, manipulation does not have to be something negative. Before you read this book, work through the entire concept of manipulation being a positive force.

When you meet somebody and you want to date them, what do you do to try and convince them to go out with you? You may ask them straightaway, "Would you like to go on a date with me?"

What if that individual says no? Do you look for signs that they might've wanted to say yes and there is an opportunity to try again? If so, what do you do?

Anything you do from this point forward is considered a manipulative action.

Maybe that person really does want to go on a date with you, but he or she may need more convincing, or made need to see a little bit more of your character before he or she decides to say yes. It is your job at this point to convince the object of your affection that you are a worthy companion and somebody with whom he or she will enjoy time with on a date.

You will need to use influence in order to achieve your goal which, in this instance, is to get a date with this person. Influencing somebody to do something that you want is the essential principle of manipulation.

So, as we move forward in this book, you will see that the art of manipulation is a learned skill. It is not some diabolical plan that is practiced by evildoers around the world just to achieve some nefarious goal.

Yes, there are plenty of examples of bad people manipulating others to get what they want. Con artists use manipulation to gain access to innocent victims' bank accounts and other information. Crooked politicians manipulate the public into believing a certain perception about them in order to gain their confidence and, ultimately, their vote. Employers manipulate their employees to work harder or do more than they should be required to based on their pay simply to avoid paying more for their services.

How you actually use manipulation when you know *how* to use it will be entirely up to you. I do not condone manipulating people to do bad things, nor do I condone using manipulation to get people to do things that they are not comfortable with or that are illegal.

That being said, when you understand the art of manipulation and how to get anybody to do what you want, that gives you an enormous amount of power. With that power, you can do just about anything you want in life.

You can have anything you want.

The Frustration of 'No'

The word no is one of the most frustrating words for people to hear. Even children who have only recently gained the ability to form words and understand language quickly learn that no is a frustrating word.

They also quickly realize that there are other ways to gain a yes. More often than not, children will use negative manipulation to get around the frustration of no.

In time, however, many people begin to accept that the word no is final and there is no way around it. That is simply not true. Almost every 'no' has an alternative yes somewhere lurking around.

If something is very important to you and you are met with a no, gaining a yes is simply a matter of manipulating the person into seeing things from your perspective and understanding whatever you bring to the table to make that no become a yes.

So let's begin by talking about the underlying theme of manipulation:

Influence.

Chapter 1 – What is Influence?

What is influence?

Influence is defined as, "The capacity to have an effect on the character, development, or behavior of someone or something, or the effect itself."

In other words, influence is the ability to alter, or effectively change, a person's or group's opinion, beliefs, actions, or thoughts.

If you can influence a person to change the way they think, the way they act, or what they believe in, then you could get them to do just about anything you want.

There are plenty of examples throughout history of people using an incredible amount of influence, amazing skills of persuasion, to bring people to their cause and effect change across a local, regional, national, or even a global scale.

You have probably heard people labeled as *influential*. As in, "That person is so influential, do you see how people just talk to him?"

Or, "The president of United States is one of the most influential people in the world."

So what does that mean? We know the definition of influence, but what does it mean to be influential?

You could probably get your child to clean his room once in a while. Does that make you influential? Are you influencing him to clean the room? In a way you are. But the level of influence, or if there is any influence in this action, is determined by the reason why your child would then clean his room.

If your child cleans his room because he is afraid of the consequences, that isn't influence. It is simply exerting power over your child. However, if you sit down and explain to your child the benefits of having a clean room (that he would be able to find toys, pencils, or even his clothing easier, thus not missing out on important and exciting fun activities) and then he decides to keep his room clean, that is a powerful influential act.

In this instance, you have applied influence to another individual to change his behavior, his actions.

Anybody can exert power over another person to get them to do something they want. That isn't influence.

A person who invades somebody's home and holds them at gunpoint so that they can rob their house is exerting power. But there is no influence going on.

Influence comes through the process of communicating, words or actions, and ideology or a belief system that you believe in and want others to understand and ultimately believe in themselves. Influence requires intelligence, well-reasoned thoughts, respectable actions, and sometimes persistence.

In the introduction, I mentioned trying to get somebody to go on a date with you. Let's say you were a 25-year-old and who is enamored with a colleague at work. You become friends with this woman, talk about sports or news or other activities family life with her at the water cooler. She laughs at your jokes, she flips her hair at opportune times, and you feel the chemistry between you two.

So you decide to ask her out on a date. She turns you down with a simple explanation that, since you two work together, she would rather not make things uncomfortable if it didn't work out between you two.

So you go to work every day looking at this woman, laughing with her, and still enjoying her company, and every day you begin to think more and more that you two would be very good for each other. You begin to consider all of the potential outcomes of one simple date.

You invite her to lunch, not as a date but as a colleague. There are other colleagues from work at this café. You sit down and you talk just like you do at the water cooler and it feels comfortable. You bring up the idea of a formal date again, and once again she shoots you down. However, you have worked through this conversation already and present all of your ideas and the possible outcomes. You explain to her your concerns and your fears, as well as your belief that it's worth exploring.

She listens to you, sees that you have very reasonable and rational ideas to share on the topic, and that you have taken your time to consider all of this. She realizes that you are not simply asking her on a date with the hopes of ending up in bed with her at the end of the night. In the back of her mind, her opinion or her firm 'no' has begun to change. She begins to consider the possibility of going out on a formal date with you.

That is the fundamental concept of influence. You presented an alternative argument or idea that was counter to her initial response, and you did so in a way that was non-confrontational but rather opened up her mind to the prospect, the idea of going on a date with you.

This doesn't mean that she is going to say yes. However, once you begin to understand influence you begin to understand power.

Power
Power is "the ability to act or produce an effect."

If you have power over another person, you can get them to do what you want, when you want. Power, just like manipulation, is neither inherently positive or negative. It is simply a product of the person wielding that power that determines its effect on the world or the people around you.

Lots of people have power and they use it for bad reasons. There are also a number of people who have power and use it for good reasons.

Just like manipulation, the word power conjures up a specific image of an individual wielding that power over others. It's usually a negative image. The image of a nation's leader standing above the sea of people, this leader having an army behind him, guns trained on citizens, is a common image of power.

How does someone gain power? There are many different ways that you can gain power. Some people take power from others through physical force. That is the most commonly understood form of power. Individuals with similar ideologies get together and when you have enough people sharing the same ideas, they begin to gain power.

We have seen the subject of power throughout the Middle East over the past couple of years. Demonstrators taking to the streets to demand their government change hands. A few people who congregate in the open demanding change for an entire nation are not going to gain any real power. They don't have any real power. They may be able to influence others to their cause and when they do they begin to gain more power.

The more people that you can influence, the more power you have. Recently in Egypt, protesters took to the streets for the second time in two years to demand a regime change in their government's leadership. Tens of thousands of people marched to demand these changes. They had power because there were so many people who shared the same concepts and ideas about what their government should look like and how their government should act.

When you have a smaller group of people, such as a family, the ability to gain power becomes easier. When you work for a company that has, let's say 100 people, you need to influence fewer people to gain more power. If you want to enact changes within your workplace, you would need, for example, 40 people, other employees, to support your ideas and to present them to your bosses. Having 40 people stand behind you when you make your demands becomes a powerful force to consider.

Unions for years gained an enormous amount of power within the workplace because they were supported by a large percentage of the workforce. Today those numbers are dwindling and as a result the power of unions is fading.

One gains power most effectively when he or she can influence others to support his or her ideas. You can certainly grab weapons and force people into standing beside you or behind you, or keeping them down, but eventually enough of those people will join forces and turn on you. When you use physical force to gain power, you haven't influenced anybody so you don't really have true power. You'll have temporary power that is little more than an illusion.

Why do People Allow Themselves to be Influenced?

There are essentially two types of people in the world: leaders and followers.

Most people tend to be followers, predominantly because they either don't possess the skills to be leaders or they don't have the desire to have that level of responsibility on their shoulders.

Most of us have more than enough responsibility hanging over us every day. Going to work, taking care of children, paying bills, looking after family and friends, and so much more. How many times have you seen things in the news that you didn't like and wished you could change, but you knew you didn't have the time to get involved?

Some people are natural leaders, or more accurately, have a strong enough desire to be leaders that they learn the skills to be able to influence others.

So why do so many people allow themselves to be influenced? One of the key reasons is information. Even though we are currently in the most incredible age as far as information is concerned, people have limited knowledge about a wide range of topics. For so long, gaining unbiased knowledge about any topic required going to the library, looking up in the card catalog the right books to read, and sifting through the books to determine if it even had the right information they were looking for.

Today, all you have to do is Google search the topic and you are met with a wealth of information, most of it biased and inaccurate. This overwhelming amount of information is both a blessing and a curse. When people have to struggle to get information, or when they are overwhelmed with so many opposing viewpoints on certain topics, they tend to be more open to the opinions of others who *appear* to know what's best or what they're talking about.

People allow themselves to be influenced because it's often easier to listen to rational, well-reasoned thoughts and ideas from others.

In essence, most of us want to be influenced so that we can feel assured that we are doing the right thing in our lives, making the right decisions, and that alleviates a tremendous amount of stress.

Just think about the last time you were influenced by someone, whether it was a politician, a musician, an actor, a friend, parent, or anybody else. Why were you influenced? What was it that they did that influenced you?

Was it their passion?

Was it the information they possessed?

Was it there position in society?

Was it their name?

Was it their relationship to you?

Or was it because you found out on your own that what they were saying was factual?

People allow themselves to be influenced because it provides comfort. Being part of a team, even if it's only the illusion of a team, provides us the feeling of comfort in numbers. It is much more difficult, both mentally and physically, to achieve things or think that you can achieve things when you are alone or feel alone.

Now, do you want to be influenced or do you want to be the one to influence others?

Chapter 2 – Defining Your Influence

What kind of influence do you have right now, at this moment?

If you say that you have none, then you are likely wrong. Almost everyone has some level of influence on other people.

Defining your influence is about defining your "sphere of influence." Your sphere of influence is a collection of people that you know who trust you, who trust your opinions, and who count on you in some way and in some fashion.

You begin to define your influence in concentric circles. Think of these concentric circles as those similar to what you might find on a dartboard or archery target.

In the center, you have the smallest circle. This is the hardest to hit in darts, but it also offers some of the highest points on the entire dartboard. In this center circle would be the people who trust you the most, the ones over whom you have the most influence. For most people, these are categorized as family or best friends. Your spouse, children, siblings, or childhood friend with whom you are still in constant communication. These are the people who would listen to you and would be most likely to follow you if you gave them a cogent and well-reasoned explanation about why they should follow you.

That is a great responsibility and a powerful level of influence to have. It also requires a great deal of common sense and restraint not to abuse that level of influence, which, as we learned, is power. The moment you begin to take advantage of the people who trust you the most is the moment when you begin to lose influence and power.

Now, in the next circle would be the individuals who still trust you but over whom you don't have the same level of influence as you do in that center circle. These could be good friends and other family members, such as parents, cousins, your aunt and uncle, friends that you get together with once in a while but with whom you don't share a great many secrets.

Beyond that, you have other circles of influence. These could be coworkers, employees, acquaintances, and more casual friends and even further away family members. Each level of influence away from your center is another circle in your sphere of influence.

This is how you define your influence.

Do You Have Any Influence?

Take a moment right now to determine whether you have any influence. In the beginning of this chapter, I mentioned that a lot of people will immediately assume that they don't have any real influence.

Now that you have looked at your sphere of influence, do you realize that you have at least some level of influence over other people? It's a pretty eye-opening experience when you begin to see the different levels of influence that you have over people.

The reason why you may not have seen it before is because when we consider having influence over others, we tend to immediately think of it in terms of getting something we want such as a raise, a promotion, or something else that is beyond our immediate circle of family and close friends.

Influence begins and is most powerful with the people who are closest to us.

But I don't want to take advantage of my family and close friends.

I have heard this statement many times when I talk to people about the power of influence in the art of manipulation. And what I tell them is what I mentioned in the introduction and first chapter of this book: influence is not a negative thing. You need to get beyond the idea that influence and power as well as manipulation are negative connotations.

Of course no one wants to take advantage of their family and close friends. That is not what this book is about. However, in order to gain power you need to be able to influence others to your cause, no matter what the cause is.

If you begin to discuss ideas, whether you want to open up your own business, buy a boat, set up a rental property, invest in stocks, or anything else, and you do so with a rational and well thought out process, if your close friends and family become influenced by your ideas, then how could that ever be considered taking advantage of them?

The answer is simple: it is not.

When you present your ideas, your ideology, or your ambitions to other people with information, facts, and clear presentation, if they support you, regardless of their relationship to you, that is of their own design. When that happens, there is no such thing as "taking advantage of them."

Influence begins with an idea. That idea takes shape in your mind. It becomes supported by research and fact finding. When your idea solidifies and is supported by the facts that you have uncovered, it molds into something more. It begins to develop into a passion. When you are passionate about something, have strong facts to support your ideas, and you learn how to express your ideas to others in a way that they can understand those facts, you begin to develop more influence.

Once you learn how to influence people, you gain power. When you gain power you can "manipulate" people to get anybody to do what you want them to do.

Hopefully at this point you can understand and realize that manipulation is not a bad thing. It is simply a tool that every single person possesses deep down under the surface to bring others to their cause and help them achieve their goals and ambitions.

Manipulation and power do not necessarily work well with a bad first impression, but a powerful and positive first impression can certainly make the art of manipulation easier to master.

Chapter 3 - A Powerful First Impression

First impressions.

When you see that term, does it send nervous shivers through your body? A lot of people understand that first impressions are some of the most important we can ever make.

The famous adage goes: you never get a second chance to make a first impression.

There is no denying that fact. If you do not make a powerful first impression, then your challenge to influence others to your ideas, or to do what you want them to do, becomes much more challenging.

That doesn't mean that you will not be able to get those people to do what you want them to do. It simply means that it will take a different approach and make the challenge tougher and slower.

A Little Story ...

Allow me to tell you a little story here about first impressions. Anybody who has ever gone on a job interview will understand what first impressions can be. I mentioned job interviews in the introduction because they are some of the most simple and relatable experiences that people have that involve influence, power, and some manipulation.

So let's talk about a man named Fred. Fred worked his way through college and after seven grueling years, earned his Masters in business administration (MBA). It took him more than 16 months to find work with his new degree and it wasn't exactly what he was hoping to achieve out of college. He ended up in the mailroom of a major firm running all sorts of menial tasks. But he did it because he believed that he would get an opportunity to fulfill his career goals and passions.

So Fred kept applying to other companies and firms throughout the city. One day, after several months of filling out applications, making follow-up phone calls, and waiting and working in the menial job that he couldn't stand, he finally received a call to come in for an interview at one of the top three companies he could hope to work for.

He woke up the morning of his interview excited and nervous. He took a shower, he groomed himself, he put on his finest suit and best tie, shined his shoes, and looked the part of a professional.

He went to the building for his interview and worked through every possible question that he could imagine they would ask. He'd been practicing interviews for years now. He was well-versed and knew how to carry himself.

However, when he was called into the office for his interview, he didn't realize that there was a mustard stain on his shirt from the lunch he had just eaten a short time ago. He also wasn't expecting to have three high-powered executives sitting across from him while they examined him and asked him questions.

He immediately became nervous, started sweating, and when one of the interviewers pointed out mustard stain, he became distracted. He began stuttering his responses, forgetting the names of two of the gentleman interviewing him, and struggling to get through the interview.

In the end, his interview was a disaster and he made a horrible first impression. Now, we won't know whether the reason he did not get the position had anything to do with the mustard stain or his nervousness or his inability to remember names. However, what must those interviewers have been thinking when they saw a gentleman sitting across from them with the stain on his shirt, stammering for answers, and unable to remember their names which they told him more than once?

People make judgments about us all the time based on the first impressions. Now, let's say in six months Fred gets another call from the same company to come in for an interview. He sits down with the same three interviewers. How much more work do you think he will have to do to convince them that what they saw in the first interview wasn't the essence of who he is?

Now, he will have to work harder to convince them of his qualifications to overcome that bad first impression and stand out among his peers.

When you make a strong first impression, you set the stage to be able to influence those other people in a more effective manner. If you make a poor first impression, then you will have to work harder, and expend more energy trying to convince them that your ideas or your qualifications are the right ones and what they should follow.

How do You Make a Powerful First Impression?

There is a great deal of debate on how to make powerful first impression. Some people believe in being calm and relaxed. Others think you should make the other person feel comfortable in your presence. Others believe you need to avoid being arrogant, but still have confidence in yourself and your abilities and your ideas.

I believe it's a combination of all three.

The first and most important key is to smile and allow the other person to feel comfortable in your presence. Do not be confrontational and overpowering when making your first impression.

Allow them to talk and share their ideas if they have some. Allow them to believe (and you should) that you care about what they have to say.

Keep your ego in check; you may have the best ideas or have done the most research into a variety of topics, but that doesn't mean you know everything. Be willing to explain your position and ideas to others several times.

Be confident. There's a fine line between arrogance and confidence. Confidence builds your stature. Arrogance drives people away from you.

You make a powerful first impression by showing people the *best* parts of your character and knowledge. You can be the smartest person in the world, but there's a difference between *knowledge* and *intelligence*.

When you balance your knowledge with a pleasant personality (not boisterous or too shy), and appear confident, but not arrogant, you will give a strong first impression. It is essentially that simple.

And that complicated.

It takes practice to learn how to give a good, strong first impression. So, practice your first impressions in the mirror. Imagine different scenarios and speak to the mirror, stand tall, smile, and be pleasant and endearing.

Don't believe that first impressions are the products of a birthright. Anyone can provide a powerful first impression with the right practice, patience, and willingness to learn.

Until you fully master that powerful first impression though, you should be aware of the people who are trying to manipulate you.

Chapter 4 – How to Determine if Someone is Trying to Manipulate You

Is someone trying to manipulate you?

It's an interesting question and one that few of us ever bother to ask. However, if you don't ask this question, then you could become a victim of manipulation. When you are the victim of manipulation, you end up exerting your energy and effort to move someone else closer to their goals and ambitions. When you are moving someone else closer to their goals and ambitions, in most cases, you are keeping yourself farther away from yours.

There are many different ways that we are influenced or manipulated in our lives. As mentioned in the introduction of this book, parents are often manipulated by their children to allow them to do things that the parents might not want them to do in the first place. One of the most common ways that children manipulate their parents is by throwing temper tantrums when they are told that they can't have something or can't do something. The parents then, in turn, decide between dealing with the temper tantrum or alleviating the frustration by giving in to the demands.

At the time, it may seem harmless to allow a child to get what he or she wants after throwing a temper tantrum. However, that behavior and subsequent surrender by the parents only reinforces the notion within the child's mind that he or she can get whatever they want simply by acting out in a negative way. This is the fundamental principle of negative reinforcement.

But you are an adult, surrounded by adults, and you might not even have children of your own, so how can you know if someone is manipulating you?

Have you ever done something that you weren't comfortable with or that, deep down in your mind, you didn't really want to do because you felt that it would alleviate someone else's suffering? If you have, then you have become the victim of manipulation.

It doesn't matter who was doing the manipulation. It only matters what the result happens to be.

Let me tell you another story ...

Megan had been working for her boss for over a year. She was a salaried administrative assistant, which meant that no matter how many hours a week she worked, she was always going to take home the same amount of pay.

Most of the other employees in the company were hourly paid employees, so whenever they had to work late on the weekends, they were earning overtime. But not Megan.

Throughout the first year, she might've worked an extra hour or two during the week only a handful of times. She was more than willing to do it because she appreciated the job that she had and the opportunity given to her by her new boss.

Yet after a year, her boss approached her and asked if she would be willing to put in an extra hour a day, half-hour in the morning and half-hour in evening to answer phones and do other administrative tasks. At first she didn't think twice about it, especially since her boss said it was just for a "short time."

Megan wasn't happy with the extra hours, but she had her sights set on a different position within the company. Her boss knew about her ambitions and had told her that her extra effort would bode well when that position opened up.

Megan's boss did not specify how long or how many weeks these "extra hours" would last. He also didn't offer any concrete promises that her effort would result in a promotion. He merely dangled that carrot in front of her, knowing that she was interested in a promotion, and knowing that hinting at it would be more likely to produce the results that he wanted.

Her boss also understood that an hour extra every day, especially at the end of the day, would be a tougher sell to get her to agree to. So he cleverly broke up the extra hour into half-hour segments, one in the morning and one in the evening. After all, when you think about an extra half hour at the end of the day, that doesn't seem as bad as working an extra full hour.

Megan was manipulated by her boss. She ended up working those extra hours because she agreed to them for 6 months before she finally addressed her boss and told him that she couldn't keep putting in those "free" hours.

When the job that she coveted opened up, she was never even interviewed for it. Megan allowed herself to be manipulated because she thought that would be the best way to achieve her own ambitions.

The Danger Zone

Are you sitting inside the danger zone of manipulation?

In other words, is there something that you want that people around you know about and could potentially use it against you to get you to do something to help them and which you would otherwise not be willing to do? That is known as your danger zone.

It is the area in your life where other people can take advantage of you to get what they want without regard for what is best for you.

Every single person has a danger zone within their life. Parents want their children to behave or to be quiet, often to not cause a scene in public. Employees often want promotions or raises. People in communities want safer roads, lower crime, or other social benefits.

Every single one of these people, if asked, would be willing to give up something of value that they already have, such as their time or a little freedom, to get what they want. This creates blind spots and it opens us up to manipulation.

Signs that Someone May be Manipulating You

There are signs all around us to indicate whether someone is trying to manipulate us or not. Too often though, we simply ignore the signs because we don't want to believe it. Below are some signs that could indicate someone is trying to manipulate you.

Keep in mind, when you are looking at this list, be aware of your own actions against others. If you find that you are doing this to other people, it can be a sign that you are using manipulation for negative purposes and in a bad way.

1. *Observe.* Pay attention to the way that people act around you when they want something. Do they change? Does someone suddenly begin calling you more often, offering to help out when they normally wouldn't? Does this person suddenly seem nicer to you? This could be a sign that someone is attempting to get something out of you or manipulate you for something.
2. *Pay attention to your feelings.* How do you feel when someone asks you for a favor? Do you tend to feel guilty or shamed into doing something that you don't really want to? People have a nasty habit of trying to lay a guilt trip on others

to get what they want. If you end up doing things that are uncomfortable to you or that you do not really want to do only because you feel guilty for saying no, then you are being manipulated. You are also being a willing partner in that manipulation. No one should do something because they feel guilty otherwise. That also means that when you want someone to do something, trying to use guilt to get them to do it is a negative form of manipulation. Positive manipulation is about getting people to do what you want them to do while also having them willing and happy to do it.

3. ***Look for temper tantrums.*** When we think of temper tantrums, we think of the young child who begins to yell and scream, pound his or her feet or hands against the ground, curl up in a little ball and cry. Yet temper tantrums can take any number of forms. The most common form of temper tantrums in adults is losing one's temper. Raising their voice when they don't get their way, calling

other people names, teasing people, and other subtle actions are attempts to manipulate people in a negative way. When you fear a person's temper, you have an increased likelihood of doing what they want just so that you can avoid that temper tantrum.

4. *The "victim."* A lot of people like to play the victim in life. Even though someone is fully capable of doing things for himself or herself, they tend to lean on others and make it seem as though they are helpless. This can lead you to feel guilty if you don't help them. When you recognize "victims" in your life, you can guard against being manipulated by them. Most people are fully capable of doing any number of ordinary tasks and challenges in life, so don't fall for the act.

The more you know and understand about how people could manipulate you, the more you become aware of the art of manipulation and its negative light. But that is not the goal of this book and it should not be your focus in life. Using the art of manipulation to get people to do what you want them to do should bring about positive changes in your life and theirs.

Chapter 5 – Monitoring Your Influence

When you want to get anybody to do what you want, you are seeking to have influence over them. As I've mentioned several times in this book so far, influence, manipulation, and power have no inherent value by themselves. What you use them for determines whether they are positive or negative forces in your life and in the lives of the people around you.

It is essential that you monitor your influence at all times when you begin to learn the art of manipulation. There is an adage that states, "Absolute power corrupts absolutely."

This statement means that the more power you gain, the more easily it can corrupt you and your intentions, turning your good intentions into poor actions.

There have been countless examples of leaders throughout history who may have had good intentions when they rose to power, but the more power they gained the less they actually care about the people to whom they swore their service. Most often in history books we tend to see these people as inherently evil from the beginning. However, a deeper inspection into their lives often reveals a strong desire early on to bring "justice" to people whom that individual deemed to be oppressed.

When those individuals began to rise to power, they often lose sight of where they came from and what their initial goals were and instead end up using their power to control others.

Manipulation should never be about control. You should not want that level of power nor should you seek it. Manipulation should be about inspiring other people around you to *want* to support you and do what you want them to do.

The Line between Manipulation and Control

This brings me to the fine line that separates manipulation and control. One of the reasons that people tend to think of manipulation as being a negative force is that it is often associated with control.

The man who storms around his house slamming doors, cursing out loud, threatening his wife because she decided not to do something he wanted is an attempt to control through fear, to manipulate by creating an atmosphere that his wife does not wish to remain in.

The boss who threatens to fire his employees who don't work extra hours or "step up to the plate" is one who is exerting his control over his employees. This manipulation uses money, as in the paycheck, to control people.

The ambitious young man who wears the fine suit, sits up straight, addresses the interviewers clearly, and is able to do so because he practiced his interview techniques and skills for hours every day for the past several weeks is exerting manipulation over the interviewers. He is showing them one very practiced, and very polished presentation of himself. It is likely not a completely true representation of who he really is, so he is manipulating the interviewers into seeing what he wants them to see. There is nothing wrong with this because he is not exerting control over them. They will still make their decision on their own terms.

If this ambitious young man suddenly decided to weep in front of them in an attempt to win the job, saying that if he doesn't get this job he will lose his home, his family, and maybe even his life, then that would be an attempt to exert control: the manipulation.

Understand the significant but very fine line that differentiates manipulation (influence) and control. You can use manipulation to get people to do what you want them to do without controlling their actions or decisions. That is true power. When people support you and do what you want them to do, you have a power that cannot be taken away.

People who gained power through control almost always lose that power eventually when enough people realize that they are being controlled. Freedom is a contagious thing. When you move through life using manipulation to get people to do what you want, always keep in mind that you want them to have freedom of choice in the end.

Chapter 6 – See through People

One of the most difficult skill sets that there is to learn when it comes to the art of manipulation is the ability to "see through people." However, it is also one of the most important skills to develop.

When we talk about seeing through people, we're not talking about the ability that Superman had with his x-ray vision. We are talking about the ability to read people, understand their emotions, and determine what motivates them. Some people are easier to read than others. Some people are more open and honest while others may remain guarded. Before you can manipulate people to do what you want, you need to understand what they want, what motivates them, what their fears are as well as their hopes.

That requires an immense amount of observation as well as engagement in the people that you want to manipulate or influence.

Understand their True Motivations

Let's start with something closer to home. Yourself. What are your true motivations? Why do you want to learn the art of manipulation? Are you tired of constantly asking for help and getting nothing in return? Are you frustrated by working 50, 60, or even 80 hours a week with no promotion the past 10 years, and barely any raise?

Or are you someone who has barely put in 30 hours of work for an average week your entire life and you want the mansion on the water, the fancy sports car, and other things that you covet but haven't earned?

This isn't meant to be a judgment on you but to explain how to get to the core of someone's true motivations. If you are a person who doesn't put in the effort, but you want the reward, then your true motivation is materialistic objects that you feel are going to fulfill you.

Now, if you had a close friend or family member who possessed this level of ideology or motivation, how do you suppose you would get him or her to do what you wanted? The most logical explanation or tool would be offering them money.

Money is the most powerful tool that people use to manipulate others. People require money to buy food, gas for the cars, rent or mortgage, and a host of other basic necessities. It is exceedingly difficult to survive in our modern society without money. And we think of money as currency, but by its true definition wouldn't it make more sense to view it as what it is: a way to manipulate?

Your boss promises a paycheck for time you put in. She is manipulating you to do what she wants you to do with the promise of money. You offer your child $10 a month to take out the garbage every week. Some call it an allowance. Some call it a bribe. Either way it is manipulation. You are getting your child to do something that you want him to do and you are using money to get it done.

Your landlord wants his rent on the first of the month. The only way for you to make that payment and stay in your home is to go out and get a job and work. You are being manipulated to work (but not by your landlord but by the basic necessity to afford a place to live).

These are basic motivations that people have. It is the motivation to survive. But what about those other motivations? Does somebody want to help end hunger or homelessness or disease of the world? Does somebody want to spread the word of God to others? Does a group of people in your town wish to raise enough money to improve the local park? Does a wife want to improve communication skills with her husband? Does a husband want his wife to be more open about the things that she wants to do?

For as many different types of people as there are in the world, there are that many different types of motivations. Everyone is different and that means everyone's motivation will be different.

The only true way to understand a person's true motivation is to *observe.* You observe by:

1. Talking to them. Ask questions. Discuss a wide range of topics. Make them feel comfortable with you while you talk to them.
2. Listen to them. Too often we tend to hear people but we don't really listen to what they are saying. When you listen to what somebody's telling you, really listening to the words they use, then you will begin to understand what motivates them.
3. Watch them. See how they act. Are they distracted when they're walking down the street? Do they tend to look at certain things in storefront windows? Does news coverage about suffering affect them? People will often say what they think other people want them to say, but their actions will rarely ever lie for them.

When you are able to discover the core of someone's desires, you will have the foundation upon which to base your future manipulation. When you understand a person's motivations as well as their desires, you put yourself in a position that can be mutually beneficial.

Success in life is about give-and-take. It is about compromise. In order to be successful at manipulating others to do what you want, you need to understand what would motivate them to *want* to do it. Once you understand someone's motivations, you will increase your power exponentially.

Chapter 7 – Recognize the 'Bluff'

I'm sure that you know all about the "yes people." They are everywhere. These are the people who will smile at you, nod their heads, and agree to anything you say while having no intention of following through with their agreements or promises.

People have all sorts of unique and interesting reasons to agree to things they have no intention of following through on. Some people simply don't want to be bothered and don't want to feel guilty for saying no. Some people may think that they want to agree to something, but are too lazy to follow through with their actions. However, I believe that yes people are simply using their own form of manipulation to make you feel more comfortable and make you believe that they are on your side.

We can more aptly call this a bluff. Bluffing is used in poker and other gambling games in an effort to fool your opponent into believing you either have a better hand than you do or a worse one. The goal of a bluff is to either attempt to win the game by forcing your opponents to fold, or getting more money in the pot when you have a good hand.

In life, when people are bluffing they are either attempting to manipulate in a negative way or avoid an uncomfortable situation for themselves. So how do you recognize the bluff?

The first thing is to observe body language. If you are talking to somebody and their arms are folded across their chest, and they're sitting there saying yes, or absolutely, then they are likely bluffing. Once somebody folds their arms over, their closing themselves off. Also, when somebody is looking down at the ground by their feet or steps back, they're creating an emotional as well as a physical buffer between you and them. This is essentially telling you that they are either not comfortable with what you are saying or do not agree with you.

When somebody tells you, "Sure, give me your number and I'll call you," then this should be considered a bluff. If it's something that you are bringing up, such as an idea for something you want them to do for you or with you, wouldn't it stand to reason that you initiate the call? If somebody were truly interested in working with you or doing something for you, then they would ask you to call them, not the other way around.

If a person is distracted when you're talking to them, such as looking around paying attention to the activities in the background, even when they said they are listening to you, they are bluffing. If someone was truly engaged in what you had to say then they would be paying attention to you.

When you are able to effectively recognize a bluff, it will save you a great deal of time and energy. It will also provide you with invaluable clues that can help you refine your approach with this individual.

Now, the bottom line is we understand someone's motivations and are able to recognize when they are just glad-handing you or bluffing, you will more effectively manage your time and efforts with these individuals, moving them closer to having them do what you want them to do.

Chapter 8 – Get the Results You Want. Now

Okay, we discussed what manipulation is, how it can be either a positive or negative force, how many people misconceive it as being completely negative, and how it can lead to power. We've also learned that it is crucial to understand a person's motivations in order to be able to manipulate them into doing what you want them to do.

Now it's time to get the results you want. Now.

Get the Return Phone Call

If you've ever been frustrated with the fact that people did not return your phone calls, you're not alone. So how do you get a return phone call?

Be direct and to the point. Getting voicemail doesn't mean that you're going to want to leave your entire life story on the message. If you want your voicemail deleted before the individual even gets to your number, then rattle off a long winded message. If you want a return call, keep it short and sweet.

Also, let the person know exactly why you're calling. Too many people think that adding a little mystery to the message will ensure a return call. But if you are direct, you are going to increase the chances of getting that return call. People simply don't want a mystery on the phone.

Be clear about what ***you can offer them***. Since you've already discovered their motivations and their desires, you know what they want. Some make it clear what you can offer them.

Always remember that if you want a return phone call, you need to be in the habit of returning phone calls as well.

Lastly, set a time for when they can call you back. Without a time limit, people have a habit of procrastinating unreturned phone calls. Say something simple such as, "Get back to me by the end of the week so we can discuss this in more detail." You are not saying that if they don't call back by the end of week that they can forget it. You're simply stating a definitive timeline.

Get the Job You Want

You may have a job, but it might not be the job that you want. So let's talk about getting the job you want.

Be clear on exactly what you want. If you want to be a supervisor at a major company, what experience do you have or will need to align yourself properly with that job? If you don't have the necessary experience yet, go out and begin developing it. That doesn't mean you have to get a job working within a company like that for 10 years. Most of us can develop those leadership skills independently of a job.

Practice your interview skills and how to present yourself as the most effective leader for the company. Practice in front of a mirror for a while until you are comfortable with your "sales pitch." After all, when you're in an interview, you are selling yourself. Once you are comfortable with your sales pitch, ask friends and family members to play the part of the interviewer.

Use language in your resume and your communications with your potential interviewers that target their specific wants and needs. That means you will need to do a lot of research on the company that you want to work for. What is their mission statement? How do they operate within their departments? What do they tend to look for in managers and supervisors? What are the traits and characteristics of these employees?

You may have to find out a little more about these individuals on a personal level. Contact them, represent yourself as someone who is interested in learning about their leadership skills and what it takes to do the job that they do. Be persistent.

Most people go into interviews or send out resumes without having the first clue about the company they are planning to work for. All they see is a position and/or the salary and send off their resume blindly.

The more you know about the company, the more you know about the hiring personnel, the more you know about your potential boss, and the more you know about your perspective new employer, the more effectively you can manipulate their perception of you to the point of getting any job you want.

This doesn't mean that you will be able to become CEO of the company right off the bat. It means that you will be able to get your foot in the door and move your way up much faster when you know how to manipulate people into seeing what you want them to see. It all begins with knowledge and information about their needs and motivations from within.

Get the Promotion

What does your boss want? Does he want the yes-man? Does he want an independent thinker who is motivated to go above and beyond the call of duty? What gaps exist within your company or department that you could fill?

Promotions are thought to go to people who have connections in the company; but a company isn't built on relationships of that nature. It is built on having the right people in the right jobs. Find out who is responsible for promoting to the position that you are interested in. Is it your boss? Is it a different supervisor? Is it the CEO of the company or president?

When you know who's responsible for the decision, find out what they want and what they're looking for in the ideal employee. Position yourself as that ideal employee. Make yourself known throughout the company. An employee who keeps his head down is less likely to get attention. However, when you get the attention you want, you are manipulating the people who make important decisions. You are manipulating their attention to you. Then, you manipulate their impression of you to be molded into what you want them to see based on what you know they are looking for.

Get Someone to Change His or Her Mind

We've all had people who have made decisions we didn't agree with. So how do you get someone to change his or her mind? The first thing is to accept their decision at the moment. Then, determine what their true motivations are. Did you present yourself in the wrong way? What can you do to convince them to change their mind?

Present more concrete and lucid information to support whatever it is that you are asking them. The more information, supported by facts, that you can present, the more effective you can be at getting someone to change his or her mind.

Also, give the decision time. If you received an answer to a request yesterday, don't try to change their mind the next day. Allow some time to pass while you research the information that you need to more effectively support your desires.

Find out how a changed decision on their part will support their motivations and focus on those factors when you eventually discuss the topic with them again. Everybody's mind can be changed with the right information and calm, reasoned approach. The worst thing that you can do is to become frustrated, angry, or impatient.

Reasonable and patient is the way to change someone's mind.

Get People to Open Up to You

Getting people to open up to you may seem to be one of the hardest things to do, especially if they are shy or don't feel that their opinions matter. This is when you really need to understand how people feel, think, and view others around them.

They want to feel comfortable and if they are not comfortable, they will not open up to you. So find out their interests. Talk about things that they enjoy. Keep it simple in the beginning and then build from there. Do not judge and don't offer criticism. Simply listen in the beginning and the more you listen, the more people will open up to you.

But how is that manipulation?

You may be wondering how that is manipulation. It is manipulation because of your motivations. Your motivation is to get someone to open up to you. That is not their motivation. When you make a concerted effort to get that individual to open up to you, you are manipulating them to do what you want them to do.

So, you see, manipulation is not inherently a bad thing. It can even create stronger relationships between people.

Get Forgiveness

One of the hardest things for some people to understand is the gift of forgiveness. If you want forgiveness, you need to first allow some time to pass after the event before seeking it.

The second is to have honest guilt and atonement. Understand why what you did hurt this person. When you understand how you hurt them, you can approach them with an apology and atonement that is sincere, heartfelt, and well-reasoned. Think it through.

Be patient and let the wound heal. Do not, under any circumstance, attempt to make the individual feel guilty for their hurt or anger or unwillingness to forgive you at that time. That will only harden their resolve to withhold forgiveness. Instead, simply apologize, let them know through a reasoned explanation that you understand why they are hurt and imply, don't tell, that it won't happen again. When you can manage that, forgiveness will come to you naturally.

Stop Abuse Instantly

People who abuse others may have been abused in their past, or they may simply be insecure. One of the most effective ways to stop abuse is to confront the abuser with potential alternatives. Contacting authorities, evicting the individual from a home, or the threat of physical force can often be enough to stop abuse for the time being.

The most effective way to stop abuse, however, is to uncover aspects of the abuser's life that he or she would not want revealed to anyone else. Everyone has secrets. When you find out the abuser's secrets, you can keep him or her from having any desire to abuse the people you care about.

Most of the time, people confront abusers with physical violence and that only exacerbates the problem. Isolate them, and find out what motivates them and use it against them.

Chapter 9 – Using Manipulation to Influence Change in a Positive Way

As you can see, all of the examples that I have presented here for manipulation are used for positive changes and effects. No one should attempt to manipulate others to get what they want in a manner that hurts those other individuals.

When you manipulate somebody to do something that they don't really want to do, but will do it because either they care about you or don't wish to feel guilty for saying no, you are causing pain for that individual. There is no excuse for using manipulation in that way.

Change is inevitable. People change all the time. That's why opinions can be changed. There is no such thing as a hard and fast rule in life. If you want people to do what you want them to do, make sure that it's for positive change to you or them. Always remain calm, patient, and willing to change yourself.

The word manipulation is a tough one to accept as being a potentially positive force. But manipulation and influence are essentially the same thing. Yet influence is considered a good thing. When you influence somebody to change their life, aren't you doing a good deed? Why would manipulation be any different?

The idea manipulation becomes negative when the person who is manipulating others is doing so for their own self-serving reasons in which they have no concern for the welfare of others around them.

Always monitor yourself and how you manipulate people around you. Always review your own motivations and desires. Do your motivations and desires benefit those around you? If not, then perhaps your motivation is not pure. If your motivation is not pure then you are more likely to use manipulation in a negative way.

The more effective you become at manipulation, the more important it will be for you to remain vigilant about your motivations, because more skill at manipulation means you will have more power. The more power a person has, the more they tend to want.

Set your limits against the corrupting forces of power. Once you master the art of manipulation, you *will* be able to get anybody to do what you want. Isn't that an incredible motivation to learn this valuable skill?

I believe it is.

Other Books Available By Author On Kindle, Audio and Paperback

The Killer Instinct: How To Master It and Achieve Anything That You Want

Winning Habits: Getting Rid of A Loser's Mentality

Conquering Your Fears

Passive Income: Stop Working Hard For Your Money And Let Your Money Work Hard For You

How To Create A Profitable Ezine From Scratch

The Secrets Of Making $10,000 on Ebay in 30 Days

The Complete Guide To Investing in Gold And Silver: Surviving The Great Economic Depression

How To Sell Any Product Online:"Secrets of The Killer Sales Letter"

How To Make A Fortune Using The Public Domain

Search Engine Domination: The Ultimate Secrets To Increasing Your Website's Visibility And Making A Ton Of Cash

Creative Real Estate Investing Strategies And Tips

How to Make Money Online:"The Savvy Entrepreneur's Guide To Financial Freedom"

How to Overcome Your Self-Limiting Beliefs & Achieve Anything You Want

The Secrets of Finding The Perfect Ghostwriter For Your Book

The Creative Real Estate Marketing Equation: Motivated Sellers + Motivated Buyers = $

How To Start An Online Business With Less Than $200

How To Market Your Business Online and Offline

Money Blueprint: The Secrets To Creating Instant Wealth

Affiliate Cash: How To Make Money As An Affiliate Marketer

How To Promote Market And Sell Your Kindle Book

AudioBook Profits: How To Make Money by Turning Your Kindle, Paperback and Hardcover Book into Audio.

The Fine Art of Writing The Next Best Seller on Kindle

Fast Cash: 9 Amazing Ways To Make Money Without Having To Work At A Job

Money Magnet: How to use the Laws of the Universe to Attract Money into Your Life

Hypnotic Influence: How To Create A Cult Like Following For Anything That You Do

Jobless Cash: How to Make Money if You're Unemployed or Just Plain Tired of Working for Someone Else

Made in the USA
Las Vegas, NV
06 September 2023